Capstone Curriculum Publishing

Countries of the World

Capstone Curriculum Publishing materials are published by Capstone Press
P.O. Box 669, 151 Good Counsel Drive, Mankato, Minnesota 56002

http://www.capstone-press.com

ISBN 0-7368-7116-0

Countries of the World

Table of Contents

Countries of the World

Skills Correlation Chart

Book Title	Reading Strategy	Graphic Organizer	Study Skill
Australia	Fact and Opinion	Using a K–W–L Chart	Using a Thesaurus
Brazil	Summarizing	Using a 5 W's Chart	Using a Dictionary
Canada	Fact and Opinion	Using a K–W–L Chart	Using a Thesaurus
China	Cause and Effect	Using a Cause-and-Effect Chart	Using an Almanac
Cuba	Comparison and Contrast	Using a Venn Diagram	Using an Encyclopedia
France	Generalizing	Using a Sense Chart	Using an Encyclopedia
Germany	Generalizing	Using a Sense Chart	Using an Encyclopedia
Ghana	Sequence of Events	Using a Sequence Chart	Using the Parts of a Book
Guatemala	Summarizing	Using a Cause-and-Effect Chart	Using a Dictionary
India	Cause and Effect	Using a 5 W's Chart	Using an Almanac
Israel	Main Idea and Supporting Details	Using a K–W–L Chart	Using the Internet
Italy	Generalizing	Using a Main Idea Chart	Using an Encyclopedia
Japan	Comparison and Contrast	Using a Venn Diagram	Using an Encyclopedia
Kenya	Sequence of Events	Using a Sequence Chart	Using the Parts of a Book
Mexico	Fact and Opinion	Using a K–W–L Chart	Using a Thesaurus
Nigeria	Sequence of Events	Using a Sequence Chart	Using the Parts of a Book
The Netherlands	Generalizing	Using a Sense Chart	Using an Encyclopedia
Peru	Summarizing	Using a 5 W's Chart	Using a Dictionary
The Philippines	Comparison and Contrast	Using a Venn Diagram	Using an Encyclopedia
Russia	Cause and Effect	Using a Cause-and-Effect Chart	Using an Almanac
South Africa	Main Idea and Supporting Details	Using a Main Idea Chart	Using the Internet
South Korea	Making Inferences	Using a Sense Chart	Using a Dictionary
Thailand	Making Inferences	Using a Sense Chart	Using a Dictionary
Vietnam	Making Inferences	Using a Sense Chart	Using a Dictionary

Capstone • *Countries of the World Teacher's Resource Book*

Introduction to *Countries of the World*

Countries of the World is a series of 4-color books designed to help at-level and reluctant readers learn about the history, geography, economics, and culture of featured countries. The series is curriculum-based and supports national standards in social studies. These high-interest, nonfiction books are written for students reading at Grade 2–3 levels but should interest students up through Grade 5.

Purposes ■ This guide and the student **Activity Sheets** included in it will:

- Strengthen students' understanding of reading strategies, graphic organizers, and study skills that will help them as they read nonfiction.

- Prepare students to take standardized tests.

- Expand students' experience with social studies content.

Classroom Management ■ This guide's general framework provides you with a flexible tool for efficient classroom management, regardless of how you make the reading assignments. It is designed for use with any or all of the books in the *Countries of the World* series. You may wish to assign the same book to several students or different books to each student. A specific title can also be assigned for independent, paired, small cooperative-group, or whole-class reading.

Home-School Connection ■ Suggest that students share with their families what they have learned about another country. Ask them to interview a family member about such topics as:

- Have you ever visited another country? What do you remember the best?

- Have you ever lived in another country? What was it like?

Strategic Reading

Reading is a process that requires an active relationship between the reader and the text. Before, during, and after reading, good readers use specific techniques and strategies to compare their background knowledge and previ-

ous experience with what they are reading. This guide suggests methods and strategies you can use to help students succeed in understanding nonfiction.

Student Activities ■ In support of this goal, this guide contains four kinds of Activity Sheets—Comprehension, Reading Strategies, Graphic Organizers, and Study Skills. The **Skills Correlation Chart** on page 1 suggests which Activity Sheets to use for each book. In addition, charts on pages 5, 6, and 7 provide teaching suggestions for effective use of the Activity Sheets.

Exploring Prior Knowledge/ Building Background Knowledge

Encouraging students to share prior knowledge and experience will benefit those who need additional background. Questions such as the following can serve as discussion prompts:

- If you or a family member came from another country, can you tell something about the country?

- What country have you heard about in the news that is interesting to you?

- What country would you like to visit? Why?

- What have you learned about a country from a book, a movie, or a TV show?

- Do you own something made in another country? What is the item? Why is it special?

Vocabulary

Building a strong vocabulary is a key factor in developing a positive attitude toward reading. The books in this series have been written to help students understand and master unfamiliar vocabulary. At the back of each book, a **Glossary** section contains definitions and phonetic respellings of key words. In the text itself, words are defined in context at point of use, and specialized words are followed by phonetic respellings. Introduce students to these features before they begin reading.

Glossary ■ You may want to use this section to preteach the vocabulary before students read the book. You might have students:

Capstone • *Countries of the World Teacher's Resource Book*

- Create personal dictionaries in their notebooks or journals by recording words and definitions that were difficult for them.
- Use the words in oral or written sentences.
- Redefine unfamiliar vocabulary in their own words.

Setting a Purpose for Reading

Help students set a purpose for reading by guiding them to:

- Identify the title of the book.
- Scan the book, looking at the headings, illustrations, captions, and features (such as the **Table of Contents, Glossary, Useful Addresses,** and **Index**).
- Begin a K-W-L Chart to identify what the students already know about a topic, what they would like to learn, and (during or after reading) what they learned from this book. This chart can be done as a small-group or whole-group class activity. Create the chart on the board or provide students with Graphic Organizer 5: Using a K-W-L Chart. Have students complete the first two columns.

| K-W-L CHART | | |
K	W	L
Pizza comes from Italy.	Where in Italy was pizza invented?	
Joe Mancini's dad is from Italy.	What are people like in Italy?	

Suggest that students use what they have written in the What I Want to Know column as their purpose for reading. They can complete the chart when they have finished the book, or at the point in their reading that a particular question is answered.

Suggestions for Reading

Here are some reading methods you may wish to use to customize instruction to your students' strengths:

Reading Methods

 Independent Reading

Have students analyze short sections of the book. Have them write questions that arise from their reading and relate these questions to what they already know. If answers to their questions are easily accessible and vital to their understanding, have students find them before continuing to read. Otherwise, students can do research later.

Using the Activity Sheets

As students read, have them complete a Reading Strategy Activity Sheet to monitor their own reading. See the **Skills Correlation Chart** on page 1 for suggestions on which strategies to use for each selection.

 Paired Reading

Have partners take turns reading aloud pages or chapters. Suggest that they tell each other in their own words the main points of what they have read. Students can synthesize their ideas and produce a summary.

 Small-Group Reading

Arrange students in cooperative groups to read the books, one chapter at a time. Assign specific responsibilities to individual group members to foster cooperative learning. For example, one student can be the recorder and take notes, while another serves as facilitator to keep the discussion on track. A third can summarize the answers.

 Whole-Class Reading

The *Countries of the World* series can be used to supplement various curriculum areas. For example, when you are teaching a related social studies unit, you may wish to circulate one or more of these books for reading and discussion by the entire class.

Capstone • *Countries of the World Teacher's Resource Book*

Meeting Individual Needs

Implementing instructional strategies that meet the needs of individual students creates a learning environment that maximizes students' potential for success. Suggestions for use before, after, and during reading follow:

Limited-English Proficiency

Second-Language Learners will benefit by partnering with an English-proficient reader who can read the text aloud while the second-language learner follows along. Point out the text's visual and graphic elements to help facilitate understanding of key ideas and concepts. For example, as part of the **Fast Facts** feature, the picture and the text information about the country's flag can help second-language learners use visual cues to help them assimilate written language.

Learning Styles

Auditory Learners rely principally on what they hear to process information. To maximize their success, pair auditory learners and have them take turns reading the book aloud to one another. Keep the readings relatively brief and have these students present frequent oral summaries to each other.

Kinesthetic Learners are adept at processing information through bodily sensations. Provide them with opportunities to use body language to demonstrate what they have read. For example, students can:

- Say and act out words in the language of the country by using the **Learn to Speak** section at the back of the book.

Visual Learners process information best when they see it. Have them use the country map and the Mercator projection to locate their country. In addition, have students use the many photographs in each book as a check on their reading comprehension. For example, after reading a section on clothing, pairs can use the photograph to identify aspects of the clothing they have just read about.

Integrating Activity Sheets with the Reading

The primary purpose of reading nonfiction is to acquire information. This guide features four types of Activity Sheets to help students with this goal. The Activity Sheets have been designed to give reluctant and at-level readers practical and concrete ways to help them organize and assimilate information. The chart below shows the specific purpose of each type of Activity Sheet.

ACTIVITY SHEET	PURPOSE
Comprehension	To assess overall comprehension, including vocabulary, literal recall, inferential thinking, and students' ability to respond to open-ended questions.
Reading Strategies	To help students identify particular techniques used by nonfiction writers to organize and express ideas.
	To teach students to use their identification of specific techniques as an aid to reading comprehension.
	To help students relate their own experiences to the reading in order to make meaningful connections.
Graphic Organizers	To provide students with concrete frameworks that enable them to use strategic approaches to help their reading comprehension.
Study Skills	To help students understand information-gathering techniques to be used in writing a research paper.

The Comprehension Activity Sheets are book-specific. The other Activity Sheets, however, are generic in nature and can be applied to one or more titles in the series. The **Skills Correlation Chart** on page 1 suggests which Activity Sheets to use with specific books.

Capstone • *Countries of the World Teacher's Resource Book*

Reading Strategies
Activity Sheets

The following chart suggests how to use and teach
Reading Strategies Activity Sheets.

READING STRATEGIES	TEACHING SUGGESTIONS
Cause and Effect	Causes can have multiple effects, as when an erupting volcano pollutes the air, damages forests, and kills people. An effect—a damaged forest—can itself be a cause of another effect—loss of animal habitat.
Comparison and Contrast	Comparing and contrasting helps students identify unstated similarities and differences (for example: Italy is a peninsula, but Japan is an island or archipelago. Both Italy and Japan are countries.) Also point out analogous relationships, as in pizza : Italy :: taco : Mexico.
Making Inferences	Strategic readers make inferences when they use information in the text to make reasoned assumptions about a point the writer is making indirectly. Point out that valid inferences are based on details, facts, and examples.
Fact and Opinion	Point out the difference between a fact (Canada is the second largest country in the world) and an opinion (Japan is the most interesting country to visit). In addition, guide students in evaluating the source of information before they decide if the information is factual.
Generalizing	Valid generalizations are based on supporting facts. Faulty generalizations are not adequately supported by facts. An example of a faulty generalization is: All countries that border on the Mediterranean Sea are peninsulas. Point out that some faulty generalizations can be made valid by changing a word or two: Some countries that border the Mediterranean Sea are peninsulas.
Main Idea and Supporting Details	The main idea is the key point of a reading. This may be directly stated or can be inferred from information in the paragraph. A main idea is usually supported in the paragraph by facts and details.
Sequence of Events	Information can be organized by understanding the order in which events occur. Clue words such as *first, next, last, later,* and *then* signal the order of events.
Summarizing	Information can be organized by readers restating what they learned in their own words. A good summary is brief and includes only the important information. A summary need not be done for a whole book; it can be done at the end of a chapter or a section.

Capstone • *Countries of the World Teacher's Resource Book*

 **Graphic Organizers
Activity Sheets**

Graphic organizers are conceptual frames to aid students in organizing information as they read. Organizers also can be used to generate thoughts for writing. These suggestions can be used with the organizers in this guide.

GRAPHIC ORGANIZERS	TEACHING SUGGESTIONS
Using a Cause-and-Effect Chart	There are many variations in cause-and-effect relationships. A graphic organizer can help readers identify specific causes and effects in a text.
Using a K-W-L Chart	A K-W-L Chart can be used before, during, and after reading to set and check purposes for reading.
Using a Main Idea Chart	Recording each main idea and its supporting details is a good way to remember what a book is about. Identifying main ideas and details can also help in summarizing.
Using a Sense Chart	Categorizing information according to the five senses helps readers absorb meaning.
Using a Sequence Chart	Organizing a sequence chart is a good way to remember the order in which events happened.
Using a Venn Diagram	A Venn Diagram highlights similarities and differences between two or more things. Comparisons should be recorded in the overlapping section, contrasts in the individual sections.
Using a 5 W's Chart	Good readers can often summarize, generalize, or draw conclusions by asking themselves questions that begin with a *w*: who, what, when, where, why.

Capstone • *Countries of the World Teacher's Resource Book*

Study Skills Activity Sheets

These Activity Sheets are designed to help students develop the skills they will need to complete research assignments. Use the following teaching suggestions to introduce each sheet.

STUDY SKILLS	TEACHING SUGGESTIONS
Using an Almanac	The table of contents and index of an almanac can be used to find specific information about a country. Have students use these guides to find and summarize information on a specific country.
Using a Dictionary	In addition to telling what a word means, how to spell and pronounce it, and how to use it in a sentence, dictionaries often give multiple meanings or multiple entries for words that can be used as more than one part of speech.
Using an Encyclopedia	Encyclopedia articles often have subheads, maps, and other illustrations that can help students locate and understand specific information. Cross-references can also lead students to additional information on a topic.
Using the Internet	Model how Internet sites can be accessed. Mention that information from Internet addresses ending in .gov or .edu is likely to be more reliable than information from commercial sites (.com endings).
Using the Parts of a Book	The table of contents and index can help students locate specific information. Some books also have features such as sidenotes and footnotes, a list of maps and graphs, and a handbook of special terms and definitions. Using another text, model how its different parts can be used to find information.
Using a Thesaurus	Model how to use a thesaurus to find synonyms and antonyms for a specific word.

Hands On Group Activity

After reading the text, assign the Hands On section as a cooperative group activity. Group members should assume responsibility for reading the activity, assembling necessary props or tools, and assigning tasks or turns. Finally, students should report to the class and describe what the activity helped them learn.

Connecting Reading and Writing

Writing an Informational Article

When students have finished reading about a particular country, they can write an informational article of their own. Encourage them to choose a topic requiring some further research. Remind them of how they used their Reading Strategy Activity Sheets and tell them that they will follow the same techniques when organizing their own article.

I. Prewriting

Students can use prewriting techniques such as brainstorming and freewriting to find and develop their topic.

Choosing a Topic ■ Ask students to brainstorm a list of ideas from the book that they would like to research further. You might suggest the following examples:

- An Interesting Place in the Country
- An Important Holiday
- The Geography of the Country

Limiting the Topic ■ Once students have selected a topic, suggest that they narrow it so that they can write about in one or two pages. For example, if students choose the culture of Brazil, they may want to narrow the focus to Brazilian music, Brazilian food, Brazilian dance, or Brazilian crafts.

Using the Study Skills Activity Sheets ■ After students have selected and narrowed their topic, make the Study Skills Activity Sheets available. Explain that they can use these Activity Sheets to help locate the information they need. For example, students can use Study Skill Activity Sheet 4: Using an Encyclopedia to understand how the information in an encyclopedia is organized. This will help them find the facts they need. Students can use Study Skill Activity Sheet 6: Using the Internet to locate useful Web sites, and Study Skill Activity Sheet 5: Using an Almanac to find up-to-date statistics. Students can use Study Skill Activity Sheet 2: Using a Dictionary and Study Skill

Activity Sheet 3: Using a Thesaurus to help them make varied and interesting word choices.

II. Drafting

After students have gathered and organized their ideas, it is time to begin writing. Be sure students understand that a draft is a work in progress. Encourage them not to worry about spelling, grammar, usage, and mechanics at this point. They will deal with these during the revising and proofreading stages.

Using the Graphic Organizer Activity Sheets ■ The Graphic Organizer Activity Sheets can help students prepare their research papers. Help students select the graphic organizer that best suits their needs. For example: If the student has narrowed a topic to The History of [*country's name*], you might suggest that he or she use Graphic Organizer 3: Sequence Chart to show a sequence of events. Another useful Activity Sheet might be Graphic Organizer 7: Cause and Effect Chart to show how one event in the country's history caused another to happen, and so on. Of course, all students have different learning styles and should be encouraged to make their own choices.

III. Revising

After students complete a rough draft of their work, they should revise it. Students should focus on the overall organization of their paper, making sure that information is accurate, clear, and logical. Remind students that they can add or delete information as necessary. Next, students should focus on improving the paper's grammar, mechanics, and word choice. As a final part of the revision stage, students may exchange papers with a classmate for peer evaluation. The focus of peer review at this stage should be on overall content—accuracy, completeness, and coherence. Encourage students to identify strengths first, and then areas that need improvement.

Using the Reading Strategies Activity Sheets ■ If students chose to model their paper after a specific Reading Strategy Activity Sheet, they should check their revised draft against

Capstone • *Countries of the World Teacher's Resource Book*

that Activity Sheet to make sure they followed the structure accurately. For example, if students used the Cause-and-Effect Activity Sheet, they should check to see that the paragraphs in their report, and their report as a whole, make cause-and-effect relationships clear.

IV. Proofreading

At this stage, students should read their papers carefully in order to correct mistakes in grammar, punctuation, and spelling. They should pay particular attention to subject-verb agreement, pronoun-antecedent agreement, the spelling and capitalization of proper names, and the correct use and spelling of homonyms (such as *their*, *there*, and *they're*). Peer review is also helpful at this stage.

V. Publishing

Students can "publish" their work in book form, selecting which information goes on each page. Those who are comfortable with word processors might choose to input their articles and print them out. Encourage students to embellish their work with drawings, captions, graphs, charts, and so forth. Cooperative groups might produce an anthology.

WRITING TOPICS SUGGESTIONS

How [*name of country*] Compares with the United States

Life in a Tropical Country

Life in an Island Country

A Famous Person from [*name of country*]

The Government of [*name of country*]

The World's Largest Rivers

The Highest Mountain in North America

The Ancient People of [*name of country*]

The Story of the Taj Mahal

The Building of the Great Wall of China

Life in the Rain Forest

Metacognition

Understanding how their own thinking process works can help some students become better readers. After students have completed their writing assignment, have them discuss how their reading helped them in their writing. Suggest that students ask themselves questions such as: What was the hardest part of the writing process for me? How did the information I read help me get past this difficulty? Here are some example problems and solutions:

- *I couldn't think of a topic.*
  The student might look back at the book and review the chapter heads.

- *I didn't know where to begin writing.*
  The student might review how the author began the book or look at models of expository writing.

- *I couldn't decide what was important to include.*
  The student might review the kinds and numbers of details the author included.

Encourage students to use self-evaluation and analysis as tools in all of their school work. Discuss with them how the entire experience of connecting their reading with their writing can help them in other curriculum areas.

An answer key for the Comprehension Activity Sheets is provided on page 10. You may use this key to check students' responses, or you may choose to copy and distribute the answers for students to check their own work.

Answers are not provided for the Reading Strategies, Graphic Organizers, and Study Skills Activity Sheets. These are designed to encourage a variety of responses as students exercise critical thinking. Students might work in small groups or with a partner to exchange papers, compare answers, and share opinions as a peer-review and self-evaluation experience.

Answer Key

Countries of the World: Australia Comprehension 1

A. 1. C Aborigines
2. B koalas
3. A harbor
4. E instrument

B. 5. It is south of the equator.
6. coral
7. summer
8. It uses its sharp claws.

C. *Possible responses:* In the Outback students live far apart. They listen to teachers on radio and TV. They talk into the radio to give their answers to questions. Tests and homework are sent through the mail. I would not like to ride the bus to school every day. I would miss my friends.

I would like to taste kangaroo. I would not like to eat insects.

Countries of the World: Brazil Comprehension 2

A. 1. samba
2. toucan
3. River
4. hammock

B. 5. C their sharp teeth
6. A South America
7. B Cars do not use gasoline.
8. B It built the Trans-Amazon highway.

C. *Possible responses:* Many Brazilians move to cities to find work. Apartment buildings add more floors to their tops. The tall buildings give people in the city places to live.

Progress depends on classroom hours attended. It does not depend on school years. Students who have jobs can come to school when they are not working.

Countries of the World: Canada Comprehension 3

A. 1. B coastline
2. E wilderness
3. C explorer
4. D sap

B. 5. They used to ride on horseback.
6. Inuits
7. French and English
8. They use a computer to talk to teachers.

C. *Possible responses:* Each province is in charge of its own schools and makes different rules. Some Native Americans live on reserves and go to their own schools. Students in northern Canada may live too far from a school, so they learn by computer.

Cars, trains, and planes are important because Canada is so large. People need to be able to travel across the country. Also, good roads and trains are important to help get supplies to the people who live in the wilderness.

Countries of the World: China Comprehension 4

A. 1. chopsticks
2. emperors
3. martial arts
4. characters

B. 5. C exercise
6. A to keep his enemies out
7. B walk or ride their bikes
8. A Beijing

C. *Possible responses:* Some Chinese inventions are silk, paper and printing, ice cream, spaghetti, sunglasses, and fireworks. Students should clearly describe the object and explain why it is their favorite.

China is the only place giant pandas live. Pandas eat bamboo. Keeping bamboo forests safe helps keep the pandas alive.

Countries of the World: Cuba Comprehension 5

A. 1. plantains
2. boarding schools
3. suburbs
4. migrate

B. 5. B capital
6. E government
7. A black beans
8. D farming

C. *Possible responses:* Havana is Cuba's largest city and its capital. More than 2 million people live in Havana. There are many historical buildings. Old Havana has many historic buildings. The Old Cuban Capitol is also there. It looks like the U.S. Capitol. I would like to see the new capitol in Havana.

I would like to go to school in Cuba because I think it would be fun to live away from home during the week at a boarding school.

I would not like to go to school in Cuba because I would miss my friends and family if I lived at a boarding school.

Countries of the World: France Comprehension 6

A. 1. cathedral
2. croissants
3. cafe
4. boars

B. 5. A has six sides
6. C paintings
7. B have a special
8. B dying out

Capstone • *Countries of the World Teachers Resource Book*

C. *Possible responses:* I would not want to go to school in France because French schools have longer school days.

I would like to go to school in France because students sometimes take field trips to famous places in France.

Bastille Day is on July 14. It was an important event during the French Revolution. Cities set off fireworks. People go to parties.

Countries of the World: Germany Comprehension 7

A. 1. A autobahn
2. C divided
3. A tour
4. C Oktoberfest

B. 5. breezes
6 sausages
7. land and water
8. sports club

C. *Possible responses:* Christmas; Saint Nicholas' Day, which honors a saint who helped poor people; Oktoberfest with eating, drinking, and dancing; or October 3, which celebrates becoming one country again.

Alike: On my first day of school I brought a new notebook and other supplies. Different: In Germany children do not have to go to kindergarten.

Countries of the World: Ghana Comprehension 8

A. 1. tropical
2. savannas
3. stew
4. traditions

B. 5. A chairs
6. B uncle
7. C English
8. B rarely eat sweets

C. *Possible responses:* Reserves are places where people cannot live or hunt. Animals live there freely. Without the reserves, many of these animals would die. They would have no where to live.

I would like to visit the reserves. I really like animals. It would be really neat to see them in the wild. Also, I've never seen some of the animals before. I would like to see how they make kente cloth.

Countries of the World: Guatemala Comprehension 9

A. 1. E volcano
2. D rural
3. B lava
4. C maize

B. 5. Mayans
6. chewing gum
7. They tell stories about families and villages.
8. confetti

C. *Possible responses:* They still dress in traditional clothes. The women still weave cloth. The men and women still wear head coverings. *Possible response:* It is important for the Mayans to be able to practice their traditions. This way they are not being forced to give up their beliefs.

We always go to my grandmother's for Christmas. The traditions help my family to stay close.

Countries of the World: India Comprehension 10

A. 1. population
2. religion
3. temple
4. turban

B. 5. B languages
6. C spicy
7. A hot weather
8. B with their families

C. *Possible responses:* Most schools in cities in India are very similar to schools in the U.S. Schools in villages may hold classes outdoors. Our school is in a city and is probably like many Indian schools.

Elephants help people do different jobs. They lift trees and are decorated for parades.

Countries of the World: Israel Comprehension 11

A. 1. C irrigate
2. C kosher
3. A holiday
4. B believe

B. 5. salty
6. Hebrew
7. kibbutz
8. temple

C. *Possible responses:* Both the Olympics and the Maccabiah Games take place every four years. *(Responses will vary.)*

Some Israelis live in a type of community called a kibbutz. Members of a kibbutz share everything. Each person has a job but no one gets paid. Instead they get food, clothing, and an education.

In a moshav, each family owns land and a house. The families combine their farm crops and sell them together.

Countries of the World: Italy Comprehension 12

A. 1. D gondolas
2. E opera
3. C Colosseum
4. A audience

B. 5. fruit or cheese
6. Rome
7. playgrounds
8. saint

C. *Possible responses:* I would like to live in Venice. I think it would be neat to live on the water. Or: I would not want to live in Venice. I do not know how to swim. I would not want to travel everywhere by boat.

Most Italians stop working for about two hours in the afternoon. They go home for lunch or sit at outdoor cafes. Many Italians rest during this hot part of the day.

Countries of the World: Japan Comprehension 13

A. 1. uniforms
2. teamwork
3. Bullet trains
4. kimonos

B. 5. A Pacific Ocean
6. C volcano
7. D large
8. B bow

C. *Possible responses:* I would like their schools because students work together. I would not like their schools because I would have to go to school two Saturdays a month. I also would not like to have to shave my head or take a difficult test to get into high school.

No, I should not get upset. In Japan, trains are very full. Special workers help people squeeze onto the trains. They push and shove passengers so more people can get on.

Countries of the World: Kenya Comprehension 14

A. 1. independent
2. dangerous
3. barefoot
4. equator

B. 5. B students
6. A all year long
7. C They carry diseases.
8. A the birth of a child

C. *Responses will vary.* Students should describe features of the animal to explain why it is their favorite.

Many skeletons of early humans have been found in Kenya. The phrase means that Kenya is where humans first lived. A cradle is for babies. Kenya "took

care of" our earliest ancestors, just like a cradle protects a baby.

Countries of the World: Mexico Comprehension 15

A. 1. A sombreros
2. C Adobe
3. C factories
4. B tortillas

B. 5. The United States
6. poncho
7. Spanish
8. largest

C. *Possible responses:* Matadors wear bright costumes called suits of light. Matadors tire bulls by teasing them with red capes. Then they fight. I would like to see this because it sounds exciting. Or: I would not want to see someone kill an animal.

Corn is used to make tortillas. These are like thin pancakes. Mexicans fill them with meat, cheese, and vegetables. Corn is also used to make a drink called atole. It is like a thick milkshake.

Countries of the World: Nigeria Comprehension 16

A. 1. D swamp
2. B Muslim
3. E wildlife preserve
4. C plateau

B. 5. Atlantic Ocean
6. go a long time without water
7. hot weather
8. life long ago

C. *Possible responses:* Hausas are traders. Some Fulanis are farmers, and others live in tents and move to find grass for their animals. Many Yorubas farm or fish. Ibos are the largest group in the southeast. Many work in government or business.

Alike: All people must earn a living, find food, clothing, and shelter. Different: The ways the groups earn their livings, where they live, and their religions differ.

Answers will vary. Stories should describe life long ago. Students' stories can be about their family's past or the past in general.

Countries of the World: The Netherlands Comprehension 17

A. 1. C dike
2. B clogs
3. B polish
4. A Dutch

B. 5. tulip
6. for breakfast and lunch
7. pump water into
8. cheeses named after cities

C. *Possible responses:* Canals are specially built waterways. People use the canals to travel by boat. In winter, people ice skate along frozen canals. People also use long poles to leap over the canals.

The country is small and crowded. When the Dutch prevented waters from flooding the land, this hurt wildlife. The animals who lived in the wet areas had no where to live. Today, there are special water areas for birds and animals.

Countries of the World: Peru Comprehension 18

A. 1. terraces
2. poncho
3. llama
4. patios

B. 5. C adds peppers
6. A Very little land can be farmed.
7. B South America
8. B There are not enough schools.

C. *Possible responses:* More kinds of birds live in Peru than in any other country. The Andean condor has a wingspan of up to 10 feet. Colorful parrots nest in the lowland rain forest. Flamingos live near the water.

I will see many birds. I will see beautiful sights from the mountain tops. I will ride a llama.

Capstone • *Countries of the World Teacher's Resource Book*

Countries of the World: The Philippines
Comprehension 19

A. 1. C typhoons
2. B education
3. C rain forests
4. A fiesta

B. 5. islands
6. floods
7. so hot
8. official languages

C. *Possible responses:* I would want to be a farmer. I would like to grow cacao seeds because I like chocolate. Or: I would want to be a fisher. I like boats and I fish on weekends. I would have fun going to the market to sell my fish. There would be lots of people there. I could see many different things at the market.

Since the Philippines has so many islands, people probably travel by boat or plane. In the United States, people often drive or fly when they travel between states.

Countries of the World: Russia
Comprehension 20

A. 1. E tundra
2. A ballet
3. B chess
4. D sleigh

B. 5. C babushkas
6. A soup
7. A warm
8. C Ural

C. *Possible responses:* I think it is a good idea. Some people don't do well at math or reading. This doesn't mean that they aren't good at other things. Also, some people are naturally good at sports or art. They should be helped to do even better. *Or:* I don't think this is a good idea. Everyone should get the same type of education.

I would rather live in the mountains. I do not like the cold of the tundra.

Countries of the World: South Africa
Comprehension 21

A. 1. A mutton
2. C tribe
3. E safari
4. B nectar

B. 5. trees
6. Afrikaners
7. provinces
8. for many years

C. *Possible responses:* Apartheid is the practice of keeping people of different races apart. The government finally made new laws. Now black and white South Africans have equal rights. Black and white children go to school together.

I would see wild animals. I would see the rhinoceros, and the zebra. I would go to a preserve with lions, elephants, giraffes. I would see unusual birds like the gompou and the sunbird.

Countries of the World: South Korea
Comprehension 22

A. 1. monsoons
2. chopsticks
3. Olympics
4. peninsula

B. 5. C harvest
6. B rice and kimch'i
7. A They don't wear shoes.
8. B to write people's names

C. *Answers will vary.* Accept all reasonable responses based on these South Korean traditions: People sit on the floor at small tables to eat. They use thick mats for beds. They don't wear shoes in the house. They cover the floors with thick paper. There is little furniture.

Alike: They are both celebrations of the harvest. Different: Thanksgiving also celebrates the kindness of the Indians to the pilgrims. The South Korean harvest festival is mostly about the crops.

Countries of the World: Thailand
Comprehension 23

A. 1. B shop houses
2. A spicy
3. D stilts
4. E music

B. 5. eat mosquitoes
6. rain forests
7. floating
8. straw hats

C. *Possible responses:* They cook outside. They carry washcloths to keep their faces cool. They open businesses early in the morning before it gets too hot. They wear clothes for the heat and hats to block the sun.

People live along the banks or on floating houses. Thais use rivers to travel throughout the country. Thais bathe and play in the rivers. They use river water for their crops.

Countries of the World: Vietnam
Comprehension 24

A. 1. C jungle
2. A delta
3. E tunic
4. B gymnastics

B. 5. the letter S
6. fish sauce
7. mud
8. work animal

C. *Possible responses:* Tet is the Vietnamese New Year. People celebrate it for at least three days. Parents don't work. Children don't go to school. People decorate their houses. Family and friends gather together.

It is better to live in the delta because this is land that is good for farming. A jungle has too many trees for farming.

Activity Sheets

Reading Strategies

Graphic Organizers

Study Skills

Teachers using *Countries of the World Teacher's Resource Book* may reproduce Student Activity sheets in complete pages in quantities for classroom use.

Name _____ Date _____

A. Choose the word that best completes the sentence. There are more words than sentences. Fill in the circle that matches the letter.

A. harbor	B. koalas	C. Aborigines	D. Indians	E. instrument

1. The _____ are the first people who lived in Australia. Ⓐ Ⓑ Ⓒ Ⓓ Ⓔ

2. Two animals that live in Australia are kangaroos and _____ . Ⓐ Ⓑ Ⓒ Ⓓ Ⓔ

3. Sydney is Australia's biggest _____. Ⓐ Ⓑ Ⓒ Ⓓ Ⓔ

4. A didjeridu is a musical _____ . Ⓐ Ⓑ Ⓒ Ⓓ Ⓔ

....

B. Choose the correct answer for the question. Circle that answer below.

5. Why is Australia called "The Land Down Under"?

   It is south of the equator.   It is at the South Pole.   It is below sea level.

6. What is the Great Barrier Reef made of?

   crickets   coral   red sand

7. What season is it in Australia in January?

   summer   winter   fall

8. How does a koala climb trees?

   It uses its long tail.   It rides in its mother's pouch.   It uses its sharp claws.

....

C. Pick one of the questions below. On the back of this sheet, write a brief paragraph to answer it.

- Describe what school is like in the Outback. What would you like about it? What would you not like about it?

- Would you like to eat a dinner of Australian bush tucker? Why or why not?

Countries of the World: *Brazil*

Name _____ Date _____

A. Choose the word that best completes the sentence. Write the word on the line.

| River | hammock | samba | toucan | Carnival |

1. Brazilian music with a heavy beat is called _____.

2. One kind of bird that lives in Brazilian trees is the _____.

3. The Amazon _____ flows east to the Atlantic Ocean.

4. Some Indians sleep in a _____ above the ground.

....

B. Read the question. Fill in the letter of the correct answer.

5. What makes piranha fish so dangerous?
   Ⓐ their strong fins   Ⓑ their large size   Ⓒ their sharp teeth

6. Where is Brazil located?
   Ⓐ South America   Ⓑ Asia   Ⓒ Africa

7. How has Brazil cut down pollution in its cities?
   Ⓐ People only   Ⓑ Cars do not   Ⓒ People use
      ride bicycles.   use gasoline.   recycled goods.

8. How did Brazil help people traveling in the Amazon rain forest?
   Ⓐ It built   Ⓑ It built the   Ⓒ It gave people
   stronger boats.   Trans-Amazon highway.   small planes.

....

C. Pick one of the questions below. On the back of this sheet, write a brief paragraph to answer it.

   • Why are Brazilian apartment buildings so tall?

   • How do students progress through school in Brazil? Who does this system help?

Capstone • *Countries of the World Teacher's Resource Book*

Name _____ Date _____

A. Choose the word that matches the definition. There are more words than definitions. Fill in the circle of the letter that matches the answer.

A. province	B. coastline	C. explorer	D. sap	E. wilderness

1. land that touches a lake or an ocean   (A) (B) (C) (D) (E)

2. land where few or no people live   (A) (B) (C) (D) (E)

3. someone who travels to discover new places   (A) (B) (C) (D) (E)

4. what maple syrup is made from   (A) (B) (C) (D) (E)

B. Choose the best answer for each question. Circle that answer below.

5. Why are Canadian police called Mounties?

They work in the mountains.	They used to ride on horseback.	Canada's nickname is Mountain Home.

6. Who were the first people in Canada?

Inuits	French	Ottawa Indians

7. What are Canada's two languages?

Inuit and French	Spanish and Italian	French and English

8. How do Canadian students learn when they live far from school?

They use a computer to talk to teachers.	They ride for hours on a bus each day.	They go to boarding school.

C. Pick one of the questions below. On the back of this sheet, write a brief paragraph to answer it.

- How do Canadian schools differ from each other?
- Why are cars, trains, and planes so important in Canada?

18

Capstone • *Countries of the World Teacher's Resource Book*

Name _____ Date _____

A. Choose the best word or phrase to complete the sentence. There are more choices than sentences. Write the answer on the line.

characters	chopsticks	emperors	martial arts	yaks

1. People in China eat with _____.

2. Long ago, China was ruled by _____.

3. Chinese defend themselves by practicing _____.

4. The Chinese language uses _____ instead of letters.

B. Read each question. Fill in the circle in front of the correct answer.

5. What do most Chinese people do before they go to work?
   - Ⓐ eat popcorn
   - Ⓑ tell stories
   - Ⓒ exercise

6. Why did one emperor begin building the Great Wall?
   - Ⓐ to keep his enemies out
   - Ⓑ so he would become famous
   - Ⓒ to give people jobs

7. How do most Chinese children get to school?
   - Ⓐ walk or take the bus
   - Ⓑ walk or ride their bikes
   - Ⓒ ride bikes or have their parents drive them

8. Where did the emperor of China live?
   - Ⓐ Beijing
   - Ⓑ Wushu
   - Ⓒ Hong Kong

C. Pick one of the questions below. On the back of this sheet, write a brief paragraph to answer it.

What is your favorite Chinese invention, and why?

Why does the Chinese government protect bamboo forests?

Name _____ Date _____

A. Choose the best word or words to complete the sentence. Write the answer on the line.

1. Cuban fruits that look like bananas are called _____.

     plantains   mangoes   yuccas

2. Some Cuban students live at _____ during the week.

     grade schools   boarding schools   kindergartens

3. Some Cubans live in _____ near the edges of cities.

     suburbs   factories   urban centers

4. Birds from cold countries _____ to Cuba during winter.

     hibernate   domesticate   migrate

B. Choose the word or words that best complete the sentence. There are more words than sentences. Fill in the letter that matches the word.

A. black beans   B. capital   C. factories   D. farming   E. government

5. Havana is Cuba's largest city and also its _____.   Ⓐ   Ⓑ   Ⓒ   Ⓓ   Ⓔ

6. Many Cubans rent apartments from the _____ .   Ⓐ   Ⓑ   Ⓒ   Ⓓ   Ⓔ

7. Rice and _____ are the main foods in Cuba.   Ⓐ   Ⓑ   Ⓒ   Ⓓ   Ⓔ

8. Cuba's warm weather makes it a good place for _____.   Ⓐ   Ⓑ   Ⓒ   Ⓓ   Ⓔ

C. Pick one of the questions below. On the back of this sheet, write a brief paragraph to answer it.

- Describe Havana. What would you like to see there? Why?
- Would you like to go to school in Cuba? Why or why not?

Countries of the World: *France*

Name _____ Date _____

A. Choose the word that best completes the sentence. There are more words than sentences. Write the word on the line.

boars	cafe	cathedral	croissants	tradition

1. Notre Dame is a famous large church, or _____.

2. French people often eat _____, or light, flaky rolls.

3. A small eating place is called a _____.

4. Wild pigs called _____ live in the mountains.

B. Choose the word or phrase that best completes the sentence. Fill in the circle in front of the correct choice.

5. France is sometimes called the hexagon because it _____.
   Ⓐ has six sides Ⓑ is as big as Texas Ⓒ is large

6. In the Louvre, you can see _____.
   Ⓐ operas Ⓑ soccer games Ⓒ paintings

7. Most French families _____ lunch on Sundays.
   Ⓐ do not eat Ⓑ have a special Ⓒ have pizza for

8. French people are trying to keep animals from _____.
   Ⓐ moving to the cities Ⓑ dying out Ⓒ carrying diseases to people

C. Pick one of the questions below. On the back of this sheet, write a brief paragraph to answer it.

- Would you like to go to school in France? Why or why not?
- What is Bastille Day? How do people celebrate it?

Name _____ Date _____

A. Choose the word that best completes the sentence. Fill in the circle in front of the answer.

1. A highway in Germany is called an _____.
   - Ⓐ autobahn   Ⓑ Schultüte   Ⓒ lederhosen

2. Germany used to be _____ into two countries.
   - Ⓐ united   Ⓑ defeated   Ⓒ divided

3. Millions of people _____ Germany's castles.
   - Ⓐ tour   Ⓑ rent   Ⓒ discovered

4. The most famous German festival is _____.
   - Ⓐ Munich   Ⓑ fussball   Ⓒ Oktoberfest

B. Choose the word or phrase that completes the sentence. Write the answer on the line.

5. The weather is mild in northern Germany because of sea _____.
   breezes   currents   animals

6. There are more than 100 kinds of German_____.
   languages   sausages   tribes

7. Greens want to clean up Germany's _____.
   land and water   castles   animals

8. For many German children, their_____ is their sports team.
   school   town   sports club

C. Pick one of the questions below. On the back of this sheet, write a brief paragraph to answer it.

- Suppose you lived in Germany. What would be your favorite holiday? Explain why.

- Describe the first day of kindergarten in Germany. Compare it with your first day of school. How are they alike? How do they differ?

Capstone • *Countries of the World Teacher's Resource Book*

Name _____ Date _____

A. Choose the word that completes the sentence. There are more words than sentences. Write the word on the line.

fufu	savannas	stew	traditions	tropical

1. Ghana has a _____ climate that is hot and wet.

2. Lions live on flat, grassy lands called _____.

3. Ghanaians make _____ with beans, tomatoes, peppers, and onions.

4. Older people often teach _____ to younger people.

B. Fill in the circle in front of the correct choice.

5. In some villages, students bring their own _____ to school.
   Ⓐ chairs　　　　　Ⓑ chalkboards　　　　　Ⓒ teachers

6. If you lived in Ghana, your _____ might weave kente cloth.
   Ⓐ sister　　　　　Ⓑ uncle　　　　　Ⓒ mother

7. The official language of Ghana is _____.
   Ⓐ Twi　　　　　Ⓑ Ga　　　　　Ⓒ English

8. Ghanaians _____.
   Ⓐ do not like fruit　　　Ⓑ rarely eat sweets　　　Ⓒ eat plenty of fruit

C. Pick one of the questions below. On the back of this sheet, write a brief paragraph to answer it.

- What are reserves? Why are they important to Ghana?
- Imagine you are going to take a trip to Ghana. What would you most like to see? Why?

Capstone • *Countries of the World Teacher's Resource Book*

Name _____ Date _____

A. Choose the word that best completes the sentence. There are more words than sentences. Fill in the circle that matches the letter of the answer.

A. college	B. lava	C. maize	D. rural	E. volcano

1. A mountain with a hole at the top is called a _____ .

    Ⓐ Ⓑ Ⓒ Ⓓ Ⓔ

2. Children who live far from cities and towns attend _____ schools.

    Ⓐ Ⓑ Ⓒ Ⓓ Ⓔ

3. When a volcano erupts, _____ flows out of it.

    Ⓐ Ⓑ Ⓒ Ⓓ Ⓔ

4. Guatemalans eat _____ , a kind of corn.

    Ⓐ Ⓑ Ⓒ Ⓓ Ⓔ

B. Choose the best answer for each question. Circle that answer below.

5. Who were the first people to live in Guatemala?

    Mayans   Spanish   French

6. What is made from the sap of the chicle tree?

    soda   sugarcane   chewing gum

7. What do the decorations on Mayan cloth mean?

    They tell stories about   They have no   They tell a person's
       families and villages.   meaning.   address.

8. What do children put inside painted eggs for Carnival?

    chocolate   water   confetti

C. Pick one of the questions below. On the back of this sheet, write a brief paragraph to answer it.

- How have the Mayan people kept their way of life? Is this important?
- Compare and contrast one tradition of the Maya with one tradition that your family practices.

Capstone • *Countries of the World Teacher's Resource Book*

Name _____ Date _____

A. Choose the word that completes the sentence. There are more words than choices. Write the word on the line.

charpai	population	religion	temple	turban

1. The number of people who live in a country is called its _____.

2. Cows are special in the Hindu _____.

3. A big, fancy building in India might be a palace or a _____.

4. Some Indian men wear a _____ on their heads.

B. Choose the word or phrase that completes the sentence. Write the answer on the line.

5. In India, students usually learn three _____.
   Ⓐ kinds of math   Ⓑ languages   Ⓒ books by heart

6. Most Indians make food with curry, which tastes _____.
   Ⓐ sweet   Ⓑ salty   Ⓒ spicy

7. In _____, some people sleep outside.
   Ⓐ hot weather   Ⓑ cold weather   Ⓒ the city

8. Indians usually eat their meals _____.
   Ⓐ alone   Ⓑ with their families   Ⓒ with their friends

C. Pick one of the questions below. On the back of this sheet, write a brief paragraph to answer it.

   • Compare Indian schools to your school. How are they alike? How are they different?

   • How do elephants help people in India today?

Name _____ Date _____

A. Choose the word that best completes the sentence. Fill in the circle in front of the answer.

1. Israelis must _____ their land to water their crops.

   Ⓐ imitate   Ⓑ irritate   Ⓒ irrigate

2. Some Israelis only eat food that is _____.

   Ⓐ fresh   Ⓑ falafel   Ⓒ kosher

3. Ramadan is a _____ that Muslims celebrate.

   Ⓐ holiday   Ⓑ temple   Ⓒ prophet

4. Culture means the way people live and what they _____.

   Ⓐ eat   Ⓑ believe   Ⓒ sing

B. Choose the word that best completes the sentence. There are more words than sentences. Write the word on the line.

Hebrew	kibbutz	pyramid	salty	temple

5. Fish and plants cannot live in the Dead Sea because it is too _____.

6. Most Jewish Israelis speak _____.

7. If you do not like to share, you should not live in a _____.

8. The Western Wall is part of an old _____.

C. Pick one of the questions below. On the back of this sheet, write a brief paragraph to answer it.

- Compare the Maccabiah Games to the Olympics. How are they alike? How are they different?
- Many different peoples live in Israel's countryside. Describe these different peoples and their ways of life.

Capstone • *Countries of the World Teacher's Resource Book*

Name _____ Date _____

A. Choose the word that best matches the definition. There are more words than definitions. Fill in the circle that matches the letter of the answer.

A. audience	B. balconies	C. Colosseum	D. gondolas	E. opera

1. special boats used in Venice   Ⓐ   Ⓑ   Ⓒ   Ⓓ   Ⓔ

2. a play set to music   Ⓐ   Ⓑ   Ⓒ   Ⓓ   Ⓔ

3. an ancient Roman stadium   Ⓐ   Ⓑ   Ⓒ   Ⓓ   Ⓔ

4. the people who come to see a show   Ⓐ   Ⓑ   Ⓒ   Ⓓ   Ⓔ

B. Choose the word or phrase that completes the sentence. Write the answer on the line.

5. Italian meals end with _____.

     pasta   cookies   fruit or cheese

6. _____ is the capital of Italy.

     Venice   Vatican City   Rome

7. Many Italian schools do not have _____.

     playgrounds   math classes   tests

8. Each Italian town has its own _____.

     language   saint   seafood

C. Pick one of the questions below. On the back of this sheet, write a brief paragraph to answer it.

- Would you like to live in Venice? Why or why not?
- How does the hot weather make a workday in Italy different from ours? Explain.

Name _____ Date _____

A. Choose the word that best completes the sentence. Write your answer on the line.

1. In most Japanese schools, students wear _____.

    uniforms   jukus   jeans

2. Because working together is so important, students learn_____.

    math   science   teamwork

3. _____ are the fastest trains in the world.

    Minitrains   Bullet trains   Subways

4. On holidays, some people wear silk robes called_____.

    sushis   tokyos   kimonos

B. Choose the word that best completes the sentence. There are more words than sentences. Fill in the circle that matches the letter of the answer.

A. Pacific Ocean	B. bow	C. volcano	D. large	E. small

5. Japan is a country of islands in the _____.   Ⓐ Ⓑ Ⓒ Ⓓ Ⓔ

6. Mount Fuji is Japan's most famous _____.   Ⓐ Ⓑ Ⓒ Ⓓ Ⓔ

7. Sumo wrestlers are very _____.   Ⓐ Ⓑ Ⓒ Ⓓ Ⓔ

8. Japanese people _____ when they meet.   Ⓐ Ⓑ Ⓒ Ⓓ Ⓔ

C. Pick one of the questions below. On the back of this sheet, write a brief paragraph to answer it.

- Would you like to go to a Japanese school? Why or why not?
- Suppose someone on a Japanese train pushed you. Should you get upset? Why or why not?

Capstone • *Countries of the World Teacher's Resource Book*

Name _____ Date _____

A. Choose the word or phrase that best completes the sentence. There are more words than sentences. Write the word on the line.

| barefoot | dangerous | equator | independent | Great Rift Valley |

1. Kenya is an _____ country.

2. The Safari Rally is a _____ car race.

3. Some Kenyans walk_____ instead of wearing shoes.

4. The_____ is an imaginary line through the middle of the earth.

B. Choose the correct answer for the question. Fill in the circle in front of your answer.

5. Who cleans the schools in Kenya?
   Ⓐ janitors   Ⓑ students   Ⓒ parents

6. When does the sun shine 12 hours a day in Kenya?
   Ⓐ all year long   Ⓑ only in summer   Ⓒ only in winter

7. What is dangerous about mosquitoes in Kenya?
   Ⓐ They are   Ⓑ They live for   Ⓒ They carry
      very large.   many years.   diseases.

8. What do all Kenyan villagers celebrate?
   Ⓐ the birth of   Ⓑ the birth of   Ⓒ the birth of a
      a child   an elephant   rhinoceros

C. Pick one of the questions below. On the back of this sheet, write a brief paragraph to answer it.

   • Which Kenyan animals do you like best? Why?
   • Kenya has been called "the cradle of mankind." Explain what this phrase means.

Name _____ Date _____

A. Choose the word that best completes the sentence. Fill in the circle in front of your answer.

1. Mexican ranchers wear hats called _____ .

    Ⓐ sombreros   Ⓑ ponchos   Ⓒ serapes

2. _____ is dried mud that people use to build houses.

    Ⓐ Straw   Ⓑ Petate   Ⓒ Adobe

3. Some automobile parts are made in Mexican _____ .

    Ⓐ pyramids   Ⓑ stadiums   Ⓒ factories

4. Mexicans fill _____ with meat, cheese, and vegetables.

    Ⓐ corn   Ⓑ tortillas   Ⓒ mole

B. Choose the word or phrase that completes the sentence. Write your answer on the line.

5. _____ lies on Mexico's northern border.

    The United States   Canada   Guatemala

6. Do not go out in the rain without your _____.

    hat dance   serape   poncho

7. Many Mexican-Indians first learn _____ in school.

    Chinese   Spanish   Mayan

8. Mexico City is the _____ city in the world.

    largest   highest   smallest

C. Pick one of the questions below. On the back of this sheet, write a brief paragraph to answer it.

- What happens at a bullfight? Would you like to go to one? Why or why not?

- What are some things a Mexican might make out of corn? Describe them.

Countries of the World: *Nigeria*

Name _____ Date _____

A. Choose the word or phrase that best matches the definition. Fill in the circle that matches the letter of the answer.

| A. desert | B. Muslim | C. plateau | D. swamp | E. wildlife preserve |

1. wet, spongy land where bushy trees grow ⓐ ⓑ ⓒ ⓓ ⓔ
2. a person who follows the Islamic religion ⓐ ⓑ ⓒ ⓓ ⓔ
3. a place set aside to keep animals safe ⓐ ⓑ ⓒ ⓓ ⓔ
4. a high land that is flat on top ⓐ ⓑ ⓒ ⓓ ⓔ

B. Choose the phrase that best completes the sentence. Write the answer on the line.

5. Nigeria borders the _____.

   United States   South Pole   Atlantic Ocean

6. Camels do well in deserts. They can _____.

   go a long time   sleep while walking   see in the dark
   without water

7. People wear loose clothes in Nigeria because of the _____.

   bright colors   rain   hot weather

8. Traditional Nigerian dances tell about _____.

   the government   life long ago   schools

C. Pick one of the questions below. On the back of this sheet, write a brief paragraph to answer it.

- Which different groups of people live in Nigeria? How are they alike? How are they different?
- Make up your own traditional dance. What story will your dance tell? Describe the story and why you chose it.

Countries of the World: *The Netherlands*   Comprehension 17

Name _____ Date _____

A. Choose the word that completes the sentence. Fill in the circle in front of your answer.

1. A _____ is a strong wall built to keep water out.
   - Ⓐ windmill   Ⓑ pump   Ⓒ dike

2. Dutch people used to wear wooden shoes called _____ .
   - Ⓐ sandals   Ⓑ clogs   Ⓒ thongs

3. Some workers in Amsterdam _____ diamonds.
   - Ⓐ mine   Ⓑ polish   Ⓒ harvest

4. People in the Netherlands are called _____ .
   - Ⓐ Dutch   Ⓑ Holland   Ⓒ Nethers

....

B. Choose the word or phrase that best completes the sentence. Write your answer on the line.

5. The most famous flower in the Netherlands is the _____ .

   tulip   rose   carnation

6. Dutch people eat bread _____ .

   only on holidays   for dessert   for breakfast and lunch

7. Windmills are used to _____ the sea.

   return whales to   pump water into   clean

8. Edam and Gouda are Dutch _____ .

   cheeses named after cities   queens   popular games

....

C. Pick one of the questions below. On the back of this sheet, write a brief paragraph to answer it.

- What are canals? How do people use them in the Netherlands?
- Why is there so little wildlife in the Netherlands? How are people trying to change this?

Capstone • *Countries of the World Teacher's Resource Book*

Name _____ Date _____

A. Choose the word that best completes the sentence. There are more words than sentences. Write the word on the line.

llama	patios	poncho	stilts	terraces

1. The Incas farmed on mountains by building steplike_____.

2. A _____ is a blanket that you wear.

3. A _____ looks like a camel without a hump.

4. Many houses in Peru have paved areas outside called _____.

···

B. Read each question. Fill in the circle of the letter in front of the answer.

5. How does a cook make a food spicy in Peru?

  Ⓐ adds potatoes　　　Ⓑ adds peanuts　　　Ⓒ adds peppers

6. Why are there so few farmers in Peru?

  Ⓐ Very little land　　Ⓑ Most people fear　　Ⓒ Peruvians look
     can be farmed.　　　 harvest spirits.　　　 down on farmers.

7. Where is Peru located?

  Ⓐ Asia　　　　　Ⓑ South America　　　Ⓒ Europe

8. Why do some Peruvians not go to school?

  Ⓐ Some children　　Ⓑ There are not　　Ⓒ Many parents do
     cannot afford it.　　enough schools.　　not believe in school.

···

C. Pick one of the questions below. On the back of this sheet, write a brief paragraph to answer it.

- Why is Peru a good place for people who love to watch birds? Describe what they might see.

- Imagine that you are going to take a trip to the Andes Mountains. Describe what you think your trip will be like. Be sure to tell what you will see and how you will get around.

Name _____ Date _____

A. Choose the word or phrase that best completes the sentence. Fill in the circle in front of the answer.

1. Storms with powerful winds and heavy rains are _____ .
   Ⓐ volcanoes   Ⓑ kilometers   Ⓒ typhoons

2. Filipino children, ages 6 through 12, get a free _____ .
   Ⓐ breakfast   Ⓑ education   Ⓒ government

3. Thick woods in warm, rainy places are called _____ .
   Ⓐ rain regions   Ⓑ rain jungles   Ⓒ rain forests

4. Once a year, each village has a party called a _____ .
   Ⓐ fiesta   Ⓑ martial art   Ⓒ sipa

B. Choose the word or phrase that completes the sentence. Write your answer on the line.

5. The Philippines is made up of over 7,000 _____ .
   states   islands   counties

6. Filipinos build their homes on poles to be safe from _____ .
   floods   volcanoes   earthquakes

7. Schools are closed in April and May because it is _____ .
   New Year   the rainy season   so hot

8. Filipino and English are the _____ of the Philippines.
   official languages   people groups   schools

C. Pick one of the questions below. On the back of this sheet, write a brief paragraph to answer it.

- Would you rather be a farmer or fisher in the Philippines? Explain your choice.
- How do you think people travel around the Philippines? Compare this with the way people travel in the United States.

Capstone • Countries of the World Teacher's Resource Book

Name _____ Date _____

A. Choose the word that best matches the definition. There are more words than definitions. Fill in the circle that matches the letter of the answer.

A. ballet	B. chess	C. dachas	D. sleigh	E. tundra

1. the treeless, frozen region of Russia   Ⓐ Ⓑ Ⓒ Ⓓ Ⓔ

2. a kind of story-telling dance   Ⓐ Ⓑ Ⓒ Ⓓ Ⓔ

3. a game involving the capture of an opponent's pieces   Ⓐ Ⓑ Ⓒ Ⓓ Ⓔ

4. a kind of sled that people use to ride in the snow   Ⓐ Ⓑ Ⓒ Ⓓ Ⓔ

B. Choose the word that best completes the sentence. Fill in the circle in front of the answer.

5. Russians call their call grandmothers _____.
   Ⓐ nannies   Ⓑ kashas   Ⓒ babushkas

6. Borsch is a popular Russian _____ .
   Ⓐ soup   Ⓑ bread   Ⓒ grain

7. Northern Russians wear _____ clothes, such as fur coats and hats.
   Ⓐ warm   Ⓑ popular   Ⓒ soft

8. Asian and European Russia are divided by the _____ Mountains.
   Ⓐ Rocky   Ⓑ Andes   Ⓒ Ural

C. Pick one of the questions below. On the back of this sheet, write a brief paragraph to answer it.

   • In Russia there are schools for children with special talents. Do you think this is a good idea? Why or why not?

   • Would you rather live in the mountains or tundra of Russia? Why?

Name _____ Date _____

A. Choose the word that best matches the definition. There are more words than definitions. Fill in the circle that matches the letter of the answer.

A. mutton	B. nectar	C. tribe	D. venison	E. safari

1. meat made from sheep   Ⓐ   Ⓑ   Ⓒ   Ⓓ   Ⓔ

2. a group of people with the same language and way of life   Ⓐ   Ⓑ   Ⓒ   Ⓓ   Ⓔ

3. a trip taken to see wild animals   Ⓐ   Ⓑ   Ⓒ   Ⓓ   Ⓔ

4. what a bird sips from a flower   Ⓐ   Ⓑ   Ⓒ   Ⓓ   Ⓔ

....

B. Choose the word or phrase that best completes the sentence. Write your answer on the line.

5. Pretoria is also called Jacaranda City because of its _____.

     trees   bus system   tribes

6. Dutch settlers came to South Africa and called themselves

    _____.

     Dutchees   Southerners   Afrikaners

7. South Africa is divided into nine _____.

     islands   provinces   countries

8. Traditional songs have been sung _____.

     only by rock groups   for many years   by gompus

....

C. Pick one of the questions below. On the back of this sheet, write a brief paragraph to answer it.

- What is apartheid? How did South Africans finally end it?
- What would you see on safari in South Africa?

Capstone • *Countries of the World Teacher's Resource Book*

Name _____ Date _____

A. Choose the word that best completes the sentence. There are more words than sentences. Write the word on the line.

chopsticks	island	monsoons	Olympics	peninsula

1. Strong winds that blow across South Korea are called _____.

2. South Koreans eat with spoons and _____.

3. Athletes from all over the world compete in the _____.

4. A _____ is land surrounded on three sides by water.

B. Read each question. Fill in the circle in front of the answer.

5. What type of festival celebrates gathering crops?
   (A) food　　　　　(B) carnival　　　　　(C) harvest

6. What are two foods South Koreans eat at every meal?
   (A) milk and bread　　(B) rice and kimch'i　　(C) meat and potatoes

7. How do Koreans keep the paper on the floors from tearing?
   (A) They do not　　(B) They eat and sleep　　(C) They heat
       wear shoes.　　　　　on the floor.　　　　　　the floors.

8. When do South Koreans use the Chinese alphabet?
   (A) to order food in　　(B) to write　　　　(C) to write to friends in
       Chinese restaurants　　people's names　　　North Korea

C. Pick one of the questions below. On the back of this sheet, write a brief paragraph to answer it.

* Which South Korean home-life tradition do you find the most interesting? Why?

* Compare the South Korean harvest festival to Thanksgiving. How are they alike? How are they different?

Name _____ Date _____

A. Choose the word or phrase that best completes the sentence. Fill in the circle of the letter that matches the answer.

A. spicy	B. shop houses	C. villas	D. stilts	E. music

1. Some people live in _____ above stores or factories.
      Ⓐ Ⓑ Ⓒ Ⓓ Ⓔ

2. The food in Thailand is usually _____.
      Ⓐ Ⓑ Ⓒ Ⓓ Ⓔ

3. Most houses near rivers sit on _____.
      Ⓐ Ⓑ Ⓒ Ⓓ Ⓔ

4. Thai boxers bounce to the beat of _____.
      Ⓐ Ⓑ Ⓒ Ⓓ Ⓔ

B. Choose the word or words that complete the sentence. Write your answer on the line.

5. Thais like lizards because they _____.

      are green   eat cats   eat mosquitoes

6. Thailand's _____ have many different animals.

      rain forests   cities   museums

7. Bangkok has many rivers, so some people live in _____ houses.

      wet   factory   floating

8. Many Thais wear _____ to block the sun.

      sunglasses   straw hats   heavy clothes

C. Pick one of the questions below. On the back of this sheet, write a brief paragraph to answer it.

- How do Thais deal with the heat? Give as many examples as you can.
- How are rivers important to life in Thailand? Explain.

Capstone • *Countries of the World Teacher's Resource Book*

Name _____ Date _____

A. Choose the word that matches the definition. There are more words than definitions. Fill in the circle that matches the letter of the word.

A. delta	B. gymnastics	C. jungle	D. rice	E. tunic

1. a land covered with trees, vines, and bushes   Ⓐ Ⓑ Ⓒ Ⓓ Ⓔ

2. a wide, wet area that is good for growing crops   Ⓐ Ⓑ Ⓒ Ⓓ Ⓔ

3. a long skirt with slits in the sides   Ⓐ Ⓑ Ⓒ Ⓓ Ⓔ

4. exercises that use controlled body movements   Ⓐ Ⓑ Ⓒ Ⓓ Ⓔ

B. Choose the word or phrase that best completes the sentence. Write the answer on the line.

5. On the map, Vietnam looks like _____.

    a football   a square   the letter S

6. In Vietnam, people add _____to many foods.

    fish sauce   ketchup   mustard

7. Vietnamese sandals have high heels for walking in _____.

    the heat   mud   rice fields

8. The water buffalo is a common _____ in Vietnam.

    work animal   house pet   food

C. Pick one of the questions below. On the back of this sheet, write a brief paragraph to answer it.

- What is Tet? What do Vietnamese families do during Tet?
- Imagine that your family are farmers in Vietnam. Is it better for you to live in the delta or the jungle? Why?

Capstone • *Countries of the World Teacher's Resource Book*

Name _____ Date _____

Sequence of Events

> **Sequence** is the order in which things happen. Paying attention to the
> **sequence of events** will help you understand what you read.

Answer the questions below. Write your answers on the lines. Use the book
to help you.

A. Reread the section about going to school in this country. What happens
from the time students begin school until they graduate? Write the
events in the order they happen.

FIRST: _____

_____

NEXT: _____

_____

LAST: _____

_____

B. The writer of the book you just read tells about the foods of the
country. A peanut butter and jelly sandwich is a popular food in the
United States. How do you make a peanut butter and jelly sandwich?
Do you put the jelly or the peanut butter on first? Do you put the two
pieces of bread together before you cut the sandwich? Write the steps
you take in the order that you take them. Use the back of this sheet if
you need more space.

1: _____

2: _____

3: _____

Capstone • *Countries of the World Teacher's Resource Book*

Name _____ Date _____

Making Inferences

> Writers do not always tell readers what they think or know. Sometimes the reader must use clues in the text to **make an inference**. This means the reader must decide what the writer wants to say.

Answer the questions below. Write your answers on the lines.

1. Reread the section about the clothes people wear in this country. Do you think the clothes are comfortable? What clues helped you to make this inference?

   INFERENCE: _____

   _____

   CLUES: _____

   _____

2. Reread the section about animals in this country. What inferences can you make about how people treated these animals in the past? What clues helped you to make this inference?

   INFERENCE: _____

   _____

   CLUES: _____

   _____

3. Reread the section about the land in this country. What inferences can you make about how hard or how easy it is to live there? What clues helped you to make this inference?

   INFERENCE: _____

   _____

   CLUES: _____

   _____

Name_____ Date _____

Fact and Opinion

A **fact** is a statement that can be proved to be true. An **opinion** is a statement of what someone thinks or believes.

A. Answer the questions below. Write your answers on the lines. Use the book to help.

1. Reread the first paragraph in the section about the land. Write one fact you learned in that paragraph.

   _____

2. Reread the section that tells about a city in this country. Write one fact you learned about that city.

   _____

3. Reread the section about the animals in this country. Which fact in that section did you find most interesting? Why?

   _____

   _____

B. Read the questions. Then write your answers on the lines below.

4. What was your opinion of this country before you read the book? What facts did you learn about this country? Did they support your opinion? Give examples.

   My opinion before reading:

   _____

   Facts:

   _____

   My opinion after reading:

   _____

Capstone • *Countries of the World Teacher's Resource Book*

Name_____ Date _____

Generalizing

> A **generalization** is a broad statement or rule that applies to many examples. Sometimes clue words, such as **always**, **many**, **most**, **all**, or **some**, can help you recognize a generalization.

A. Answer the questions below. Write your answers on the lines. Use the book to help.

1. Reread the section about sports in this country. Find one generalization. Write it on the line below. Circle the clue word that helped you find it.

_____

2. Reread the section about holidays and celebrations. List three events people celebrate. How do people in this country feel about holidays?

   EVENT 1: _____

   EVENT 2: _____

   EVENT 3: _____

   GENERALIZATION:_____

3. Reread the section that describes a big city in this country. Write three things you might find in this city. Then form a generalization about big cities.

   EXAMPLE 1:_____

   EXAMPLE 2: _____

   EXAMPLE 3: _____

   GENERALIZATION:_____

B. How did generalizing help you understand what you read? Write your answer on the back of this sheet.

Name _____ Date _____

Cause and Effect

A **cause** is why something happens. An **effect** is what happens. Sometimes clue words such as **because** can help you recognize cause and effect.

A. Answer the questions below. Write your answers on the lines. Use the book to help you.

1. Reread the section about the country's flag.
   EFFECT: What does the flag look like? _____

   _____

   CAUSE: Why did the people design their flag that way? _____

   _____

2. Reread the section about life at home.
   EFFECT: What is something that people do at home in this country?

   _____

   CAUSE: Why do people spend their time this way? _____

   _____

3. Reread the section about clothing.
   EFFECT: What types of clothes do people wear in this country?

   _____

   CAUSE: Why do people wear different types of clothes?

   _____

B. Think about the types of clothes you wear. Why do you dress this way? Write two sentences to show the cause and effect.

   EFFECT: What types of clothes do you wear? _____

   CAUSE: Why do you dress this way? _____

Capstone • *Countries of the World* Teacher's Resource Book

Name _____ Date _____

Main Idea and Supporting Details

> The **main idea** is the most important idea in a paragraph or section. Other sentences in the paragraph or section give **supporting details**. Supporting details tell more about the main idea. The main idea may be stated in a single sentence. Sometimes the main idea is not stated. Then readers must look for clues to decide what the main idea is.

A. Answer the questions below. Write your answers on the lines. Use the book to help you.

1. Reread the section about the land of this country. Write a sentence to tell what you think is the main idea of the section.

_____

What are three important supporting details in this section?

DETAIL 1: _____

DETAIL 2: _____

DETAIL 3: _____

2. Reread the first two paragraphs in the section about holidays. Write a sentence that tells the main idea of the section.

_____

What are three important supporting details in this section?

DETAIL 1: _____

DETAIL 2: _____

DETAIL 3: _____

B. Reread the section about animals. Is the main idea of the paragraph stated in a sentence?_____ If yes, write the sentence on the line. If no, write your own main idea sentence.

_____

Capstone • *Countries of the World Teacher's Resource Book*

Name _____ Date _____

Comparison and Contrast

> A **comparison** tells how things are alike. A **contrast** tells how they are different.

A. Answer the questions below. Write your answers on the lines. Use the book to help you.

1. Reread the section about schools. Compare and contrast the schools in this country with schools in the United States. How are they alike? How are they different?

   ALIKE: _____

   _____

   DIFFERENT: _____

   _____

2. Reread the section about sports. Compare and contrast two of the sports you read about.

   What sports did you choose? _____ and _____

   How are they alike? _____

   _____

   How are they different? _____

   _____

B. Think of another country you have learned about. Compare and contrast it with the country you just read about.

   How are the countries alike? _____

   _____

   How are they different? _____

   _____

Capstone • *Countries of the World Teacher's Resource Book*

Name_____ Date _____

Summarizing

> **Summarizing** helps readers to recognize the most important ideas in what they read. When you summarize, you tell the **main idea** and give some **supporting details**. Your summary should be in your own words.

Answer the questions below. Write your answers on the lines. Use the book to help you.

A. Reread the section about the land. Follow these steps to summarize the section.

1. The main idea of the section is found in its title. What is the title of this

   section? _____

2. Add your own words to make the title into a complete sentence. Write

   this main idea sentence. _____

   _____

3. What are the supporting details in this section? Retell these details in

   your own words. _____

   _____

   _____

   _____

B. Reread your favorite section of the book. Write a summary of the section on the back of this sheet. Use what you have done above in Part A as a guide.

Name _____ Date _____

Using the 5 W's

Asking the questions **who**, **what**, **where**, **when**, and **why** can help you understand what you read. It can also help you to organize research information.

A. Choose one of the topics below from the book you are reading. Find information about the topic in the correct section of the book. Use the 5 W's chart on this sheet to help you organize the information. You may not be able to find answers to each of the 5 W's.

TOPIC SUGGESTION	LOOK IN YOUR BOOK
What do people eat?	Section on Food
What sports do people play?	Section on Sports
What animals live in the country?	Section on Animals

MY TOPIC: _____

Who?	
What?	
Where?	
When?	
Why?	

B. You can use a 5 W's chart to help you take notes for a research paper. How is the chart helpful? Use the back of this sheet for your answer.

Capstone • *Countries of the World Teacher's Resource Book*

Countries of the World

Name _____ Date _____

Using a Main Idea Chart

A **Main Idea Chart** can help you to focus on the most important idea in a paragraph or section. You can also use this chart to find **supporting details**. Supporting details tell about the main idea. When you write, you can organize your ideas in a Main Idea Chart. This can help you decide which details are the most important to include.

A. Find the page in your book that tells about the country's cities. Reread the paragraphs about the most famous city. Then follow these steps:

- Write the main idea of the section in the top box.
- Write supporting details in the boxes below. You do not need to fill in every box.

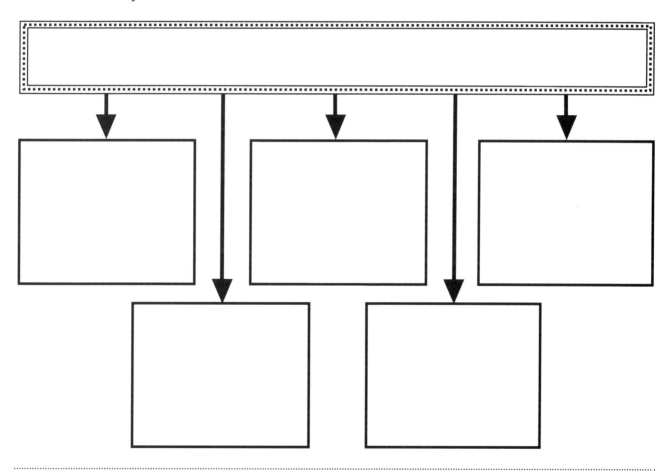

B. Think of other towns and cities you have visited or read about. Which is your favorite? Why? Copy the Main Idea Chart onto the back of this sheet. Use it to outline your ideas.

Name _____ Date _____

Using a Sequence Chart

> A story describes events that occur in a certain **order**. A **Sequence Chart** can help you keep the events in order. When you write, use a Sequence Chart to help plan the order in which to tell about your topic.

A. Reread the **Hands On** section on page 22. The author tells you how to do something. Write the steps in the chart. List the steps in order. Include only the most important steps. You do not have to fill all the boxes.

Sequence Chart for

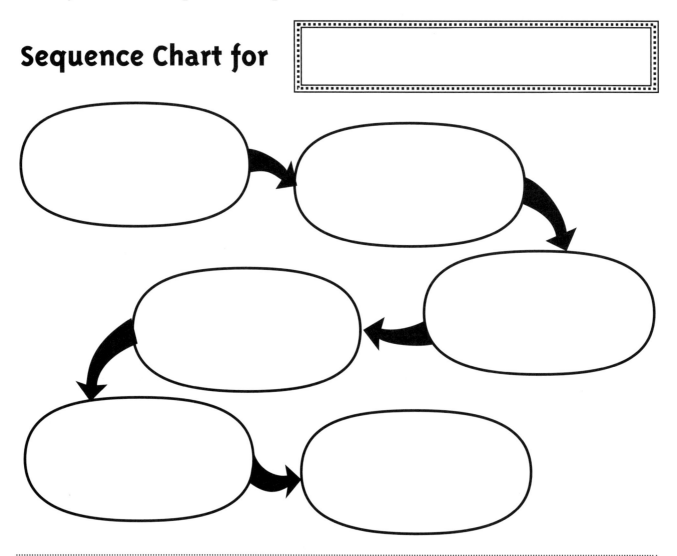

B. Think of a game that you like to play. On the back of this sheet, make a Sequence Chart. Use the chart to write what happens when you play the game. Be sure the events are listed in order.

Capstone • *Countries of the World Teacher's Resource Book*

Name _____ Date _____

Using a Venn Diagram

A **Venn Diagram** can help you to compare and contrast two different things. The part of the diagram where the circles overlap tells how the two things are alike. The parts that do not overlap tell how the two things are different.

Reread the section about animals. Choose two animals that live in the country. Compare and contrast them. Or, compare and contrast one of the animals with another animal you know. Write the names of the two animals you choose in the boxes below. Use the Venn Diagram to show how the animals are alike and different.

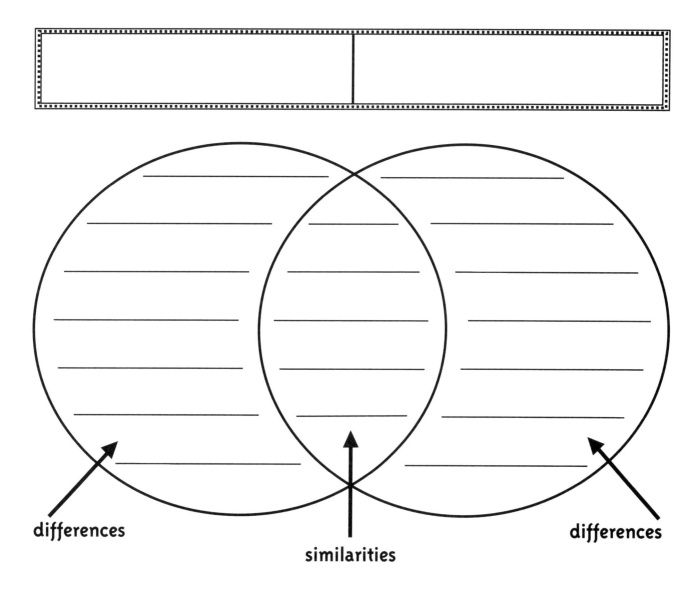

differences

similarities

differences

Name _____ Date _____

Using a K-W-L Chart

Good readers organize their thoughts before, while, and after they read.
A **K-W-L** chart will help you to do this.

Before you read, write what you already **K**now about the country in the first column. In the second column, write what you **W**ant to learn. After you read, write what you **L**earned in the last column.

K	W	L

Capstone • *Countries of the World Teacher's Resource Book*

Name _____ Date _____

Using a Sense Chart

> We get information from the world around us by using our senses. We **see**, **hear**, **feel**, **smell**, and **taste**.

A. Think about what you have read about people in this country. What do the people see, hear, feel, smell, and taste? Write your answers in the Sense Chart. You do not have to fill in all the triangles.

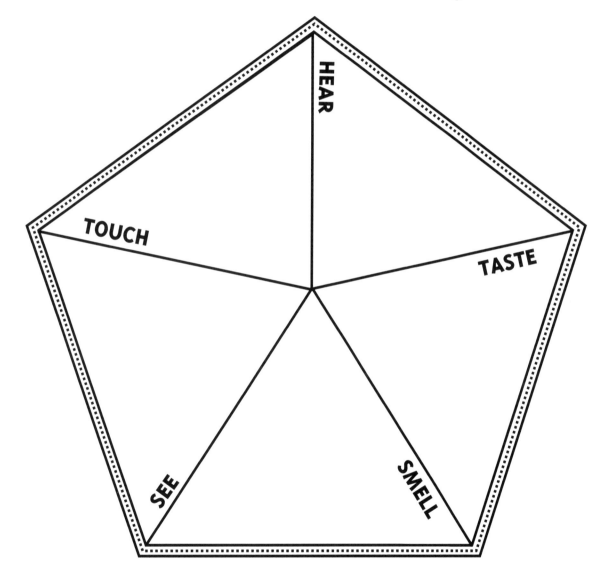

B. How does the Sense Chart help you understand life in the country you read about? Write your answer on the back of this sheet.

Name _____ Date _____

Using a Cause-and-Effect Chart

A **cause** is why something happens. An **effect** is what happens. When you read, use a **Cause-and-Effect Chart** to keep track of events and their causes. When you write, use a Cause-and-Effect Chart to organize information.

A. A country's landscape has a strong effect on how people live. For example, the city of Venice has canals instead of roads. The effect is that people ride in boats instead of cars.

Reread page 4. Think about the landscape of the country you read about. Are there mountains, rivers, deserts, or rain forests? Is it hot or cold? In each Cause box below, write one feature of the landscape. In the Effect box next to it, write its effect on how people live. You do not have to fill all the boxes.

CAUSE: Landscape of the Country	➤	EFFECT: How the People Live
	➤	
	➤	
	➤	
	➤	
	➤	
	➤	

Capstone • Countries of the World Teacher's Resource Book

Name _____ Date _____

Using the Parts of a Book

> If you know the parts of a book, you can find information more easily. Some parts of the book you just read are:
>   **Title Page**: tells the name of the book, the author, and the publisher
>   **Table of Contents**: lists all the parts of the book in order
>   **Fast Facts**: gives basic information about the country
>   **Words to Know**: defines unfamiliar words

A. Read the questions. Write your answer on the line. Use the book to help you.

1. Who is the author of the book? _____

    Where did you find that information? _____

2. On what page can you find a map of the country?_____

    How do you know? _____

3. What does the country's flag look like? _____

    Where did you find that information? _____

4.   Choose two words from Words to Know. Use each word in a sentence.

    _____

    _____

5. How do you say "thank you" in the language of this country?

    _____

    In what section of the book did you find this information? _____

    _____

....

B. Choose a book that you use in class. Compare and contrast the parts of that book with the one you just read. How are they the same? How are they different? Write your answers on the back of this sheet.

Capstone • Countries of the World Teacher's Resource Book

Name _____ Date _____

Using a Dictionary

> The **dictionary** gives **definitions** of words. It also helps you to **pronounce** words. You can use a dictionary to find out if a word is a **noun**, a **verb**, an **adjective**, or an **adverb**. These are called **parts of speech.**

A. Look at this dictionary entry. Then use it to answer the questions.

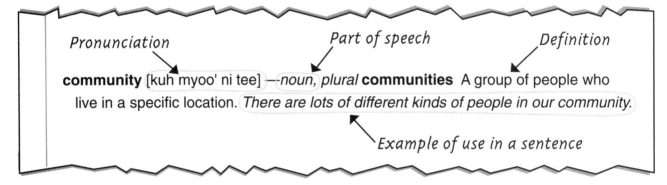

Pronunciation   Part of speech   Definition

community [kuh myoo' ni tee] —-*noun, plural* **communities** A group of people who live in a specific location. *There are lots of different kinds of people in our community.*

Example of use in a sentence

1. What part of speech is the word *community*? _____

2. Write a sentence that tells about more than one community. Use the plural in your sentence. _____

B. Use the classroom dictionary to look up the word *culture*. Read the questions below. Write your answers on the lines.

3. How many different definitions for *culture* are there? _____

4. Which definition of *culture* best describes the people you read about? Why? _____

5. What part of speech was culture in the definition you chose? _____

C. Reread about sports in your book. Find three words that you cannot easily define. Write each word on the back of this sheet. Look up each word in the dictionary. Use each word in a sentence of your own.

Name _____ Date _____

Using a Thesaurus

> A **thesaurus** can help you find words with the same or almost the same meaning. These words are called **synonyms**. A thesaurus also can help you find words that have opposite meanings. These words are called **antonyms.**

A. Use the thesaurus in your classroom to answer the questions. Write your answers on the lines.

1. What are some synonyms of *food*? _____

2. What are some synonyms of *home*? _____

   Write a sentence about the homes in the country you read about. Use

   one of the synonyms of *home* in your sentence. _____

   _____

3. What are some antonyms of *native*? _____

4. Read the sentence: *The Inuits are native to Canada.* Which antonym is the most opposite in meaning to *native* in this sentence? Explain your choice.

   _____

   _____

5. Use one of the antonyms for *native* in a sentence of your own. _____

   _____

   _____

B. Reread the first paragraph in the section on holidays in your book. Choose three words in the paragraph. Find a synonym for each. On the back of this sheet, rewrite the paragraph using these synonyms.

Compare your paragraph with the one in the chapter. Then tell how you think using a thesaurus can help with your writing. Use the back of this sheet to write your answer.

Name _____ Date _____

Using the Encyclopedia

> An **encyclopedia** is arranged in **alphabetical order**. The topic Countries would appear in Volume 2. *Cou* comes after *Cam* and before *Ele* in alphabetical order.

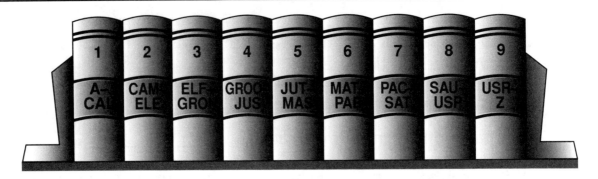

A. Write your answers on the lines.

1. What country did you just read about? _____

   Which volume will have information about it? _____

2. Look on the back cover of the book you just read. Choose another

   country from the series. What country did you choose? _____

   Which volume will have information about it? _____

B. An encyclopedia has **guide words** at the top of each page. They tell the first topic on the left-hand page and the last topic on the right-hand page. Look at the guide words below. Between which guide words would you find each topic? Fill in the letter that matches the guide words.

A. Impatiens/Isthmus	B. Atlanta/Atlas	C. Istanbul/Ivy	D. Alamo/Amber

3. Atlantic Ocean   Ⓐ Ⓑ Ⓒ Ⓓ   4. India   Ⓐ Ⓑ Ⓒ Ⓓ

5. Amazon River   Ⓐ Ⓑ Ⓒ Ⓓ   6. Italy   Ⓐ Ⓑ Ⓒ Ⓓ

C. What else would you like to learn about your country? What volume of the encyclopedia would you use? What guide words helped you to find your topic? Use the back of this sheet to write your answer.

Capstone • *Countries of the World Teacher's Resource Book*

Name _____ Date _____

Using an Almanac

An **almanac** is a book that is published once a year. It gives facts about many topics. Some topics are news events, weather, nature, geography, and sports. Some of the facts are new each year. Some are not. Many of the facts are arranged in charts or lists.

A. Use an almanac to answer the questions below. Write your answers on the lines.

1. Use the index of the almanac. On what page(s) can you find information about the country you just read about? _____

2. What kinds of information did you find? _____

   _____

3. Look in the sports section of the almanac. Were the Olympics ever held in the country you read about? _____

   If they were, what years were they held there?_____

B. Look at the section about the countries of the world. Find the country you just read about. Write your answers on the lines.

4. What is the population of the country? _____

5. What are two of the main industries of the country? _____

   Read about the history of the country. Write two interesting facts that you learned.

6. _____

7. _____

C. Look for information about weather and climate. Find three facts about the weather or climate in the country you read about. Write the facts on the back of this sheet.

Countries of the World

Name _____ Date _____

Using the Internet

> You can use the **Internet** to help you research a topic. A **home page** for a site about your topic will have much information. Use that information to narrow your topic as you do research.

A. These steps will help you learn how to narrow an Internet search. Log on to the Internet. Type in the following address: **http://www.wtg-online.com**.

1. What is the title of the home page? _____

2. Look at the map on your screen. List three regions of the world that interest you.

_____

_____

_____

3. Which region interests you the most? _____
   Click on that region.

4. Which country interests you the most? _____
   Click on that country.

5. Look at the box that says "Travel Information." Click on the arrow to see other choices. What type of information would you like?

_____

   Click on the word for that type of information.

....

B. Look at the list of Internet sites in the back of your book. Log onto one of these sites or **http://www.un.org**. Choose a topic to research on the home page. Narrow your topic. Use what you have done above in Part A as a guide. On the back of this sheet, write the name of your topic. Then write three important facts that you discovered about your topic.

Capstone • *Countries of the World Teacher's Resource Book*